Cambridge Discovery Education™
▶ INTERACTIVE READERS

Series editor: Bob Hastings

THE CITY EXPERIMENT
REBUILDING GREENSBURG, KANSAS

A2+

Theo Walker

CAMBRIDGE UNIVERSITY PRESS

Discovery EDUCATION

CAMBRIDGE UNIVERSITY PRESS
Cambridge, New York, Melbourne, Madrid, Cape Town,
Singapore, São Paulo, Delhi, Mexico City

Cambridge University Press
32 Avenue of the Americas, New York, NY 10013-2473, USA

www.cambridge.org
Information on this title: www.cambridge.org/9781107622562

© Cambridge University Press 2014

This publication is in copyright. Subject to statutory exception and to the provisions of relevant collective licensing agreements, no reproduction of any part may take place without the written permission of Cambridge University Press.

First published 2014

Printed in Hong Kong, China, by Golden Cup Printing Company Limited

A catalog record for this publication is available from the British Library.

Library of Congress Cataloging-in-Publication Data

Walker, Theo.
  The city experiment : rebuilding Greensburg, Kansas / Theo Walker.
      pages cm. -- (Cambridge discovery interactive readers)
  ISBN 978-1-107-62256-2 (pbk. : alk. paper)
  1. Urban renewal--Kansas--Greensburg--Juvenile literature. 2. Tornado damage--Kansas--Greensburg--Juvenile literature. 3. English language--Textbooks for foreign speakers. 4. Readers (Elementary) I. Title.

HT177.G74W35 2013
307.3'41609769695--dc23

                              2013016508

ISBN 978-1-107-62256-2

Additional resources for this publication at www.cambridge.org

Cambridge University Press has no responsibility for the persistence or accuracy of URLs for external or third-party Internet Web sites referred to in this publication and does not guarantee that any content on such Web sites is, or will remain, accurate or appropriate.

Layout services, art direction, book design, and photo research: Q2ABillSMITH GROUP
Editorial services: Hyphen S.A.
Audio production: CityVox, New York
Video production: Q2ABillSMITH GROUP

Contents

Before You Read: Get Ready! 4

CHAPTER 1
What a Tornado Can Do 6

CHAPTER 2
Thinking in New Ways 10

CHAPTER 3
Green is the Color of Life 12

CHAPTER 4
An Exciting Place to Live 16

CHAPTER 5
What Do You Think? 20

After You Read 22

Answer Key 24

Glossary

Before You Read: Get Ready!

A big tornado hit the town of Greensburg, Kansas. A strong tornado can destroy buildings and that is what happened to most of Greensburg. So, people had to build a new town. In the new town there were special buildings called eco-homes. Wind turbines were built to make electricity.

Words to Know

Complete the sentences with the correct words.

tornado    destroy    eco-home    wind turbines

1. _____ can make electricity for a city.
2. A _____ is a strong storm that moves in a circle.
3. An _____ is a special kind of house that stays colder in the summer and warmer in the winter.
4. Sometimes the weather can _____ buildings.

Words to Know

Read the paragraphs. Then complete the sentences with the correct highlighted words.

After the tornado, Greensburg was built again as a "green" town. It's a town that uses less energy or "clean" energy. Wind turbines give us clean energy. This is ecological, good for our environment, the world we live in.

Recycling is another way to be green. Recycling means using old things again. For example, we can put old newspapers inside the walls of a house for insulation. Insulation stops cold air from coming into the house. So the house is warmer in winter, and energy is saved. This is an example of "green" building.

1. The _____ is the natural world in which people and animals live.
2. _____ is using things like glass, plastic, and paper again.
3. _____ can stop heat from leaving a building.
4. Wind farms are an example of clean _____.
5. _____ living is a way to take better care of the world.
6. Clean energy is _____ and good for the plants, animals, and people in the world.

PREDICT

How is Greensburg now a "green" town? Read on to check your answers.

CHAPTER 1

What a Tornado Can Do

ON MAY 4, 2007, THE PEOPLE OF GREENSBURG, KANSAS, LEARNED THAT A TORNADO WAS GOING TO HIT THEIR TOWN.

That evening, the first thing that the people of Greensburg saw was a thunderstorm coming closer. Then they began to hear the loud noise a tornado makes. The noise became louder, and the wind was very strong. People were afraid. Some of them lay down on the floor of their houses. Others ran quickly to their tornado shelters, special rooms below their houses. At 9:45 p.m. the tornado hit the town. It was the strongest kind of tornado. It had winds of 330 kilometers per hour. It was 2.7 kilometers wide, wider than the town of Greensburg.

The town was hit very hard, and 95 percent of the buildings were destroyed. Houses, stores, and offices were broken up into small pieces called rubble. Some buildings and cars were carried away by the wind.

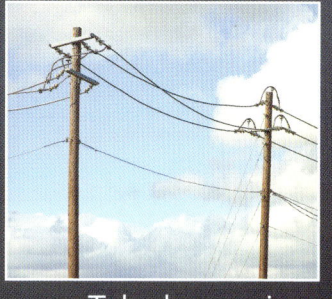

Telephone wires

The tornado caused[1] many other problems. Electricity and telephone wires were broken. People could not talk to the rest of the world outside the town. The hospital was partly destroyed, and two schools were completely destroyed.

What about the people? Of the 1,400 people who lived in Greensburg, 11 were killed by the tornado. Many people were hurt by falling rubble. Other people were caught inside destroyed houses and stores. They could not get out until others came to dig[2] them out.

[1] **cause:** make something happen, especially something bad
[2] **dig:** find and move something from under rubble, the ground, etc.

No one could live in the town after that. Almost all of the houses and businesses were destroyed. For a week, everyone in Greensburg went to live somewhere else. The town was empty. Then some people began to return to Greensburg to rebuild[3] their town. But they had nothing. They needed food, clean water, and clothes. A few days after the tornado, the President of the United States, George W. Bush, came to visit to try to help cheer up[4] the people of Greensburg. People from other areas of the United States and from other countries began to send food and other things that the town needed. These volunteers, people from many different places, came to Greensburg to work and to help rebuild the town.

[3] **rebuild:** build again
[4] **cheer up:** make someone feel happier

Video Quest

The Greensburg Tornado

Watch this video about the tornado that hit Greensburg, Kansas, USA. How big was it? How fast was the tornado's wind?

The tornado destroyed Greensburg and changed the lives of everyone who lived there. Some people never returned to their town because they were afraid to come back. These people thought that another tornado might come and destroy the town again. After all, Kansas is a place where there are tornadoes almost every year. But most of the people of Greensburg did return to rebuild their town. When these people arrived home, they did not have a place to live. Their homes were completely destroyed. Where could they live? This is the story of how the people of Greensburg rebuilt their town.

Volunteers helping rebuild the town

CHAPTER 2

Thinking in New Ways

AFTER THE TORNADO, MANY PEOPLE IN GREENSBURG DECIDED TO REBUILD THEIR TOWN IN A DIFFERENT WAY.

A week after the destruction[5] of Greensburg, many people returned to the area. They had meetings to talk about their city. Some people had an exciting idea. They wanted to rebuild Greensburg to make it better than it was before the tornado. They wanted to rebuild the town to make it "green." They wanted to save **energy** and protect[6] the environment.

Most of the people of Greensburg agreed to rebuild their town "green." A **law** was made that many buildings had to be "green." But "green building" is not cheap or easy, so the people of Greensburg needed a lot of money and help.

---

[5] **destruction:** when something is destroyed
[6] **protect:** keep someone or something safe from something dangerous or bad

Many people everywhere heard about the destruction of Greensburg. Television, radio, the Internet, newspapers, and magazines told the story in words, pictures, and videos.

A group of people called GreensburgGreenTown set up a Web site to show what was happening in their town. People from all round the world now knew that Greensburg needed help to rebuild. The Web site was a way for the people of Greensburg to tell the world about their plan; the plan to make their new town an example of the best "green" **architecture** and **ecological** thinking. People sent money and other things to help.

Greensburg was going to become a very new and different place to live!

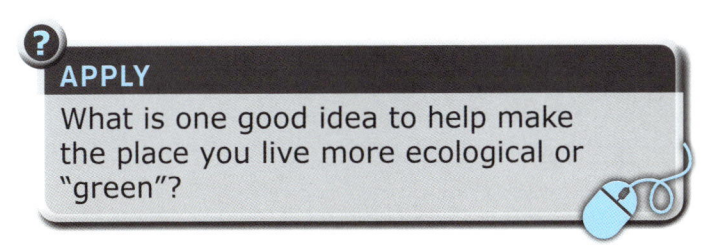

APPLY
What is one good idea to help make the place you live more ecological or "green"?

CHAPTER 3

Green is the Color of Life

FOUR WAYS THAT THE PEOPLE OF GREENSBURG MADE THEIR TOWN "GREEN."

Many people had different ideas for a "green" Greensburg. Here are four important ideas: ecological streetlights; a wind farm for making cheap energy; eco-homes for the people of the town and for tourists, too; and the idea of the students of architecture at the University of Kansas to build a "green" building in Greensburg.

In 2009, Greensburg was the first city in the United States to use ecological streetlights. These streetlights are 70 percent cheaper than the streetlights that the town used before the tornado. The new ecological streetlights also save 40 percent more energy than the older streetlights. And 99 percent of these streetlights can be recycled.

Streetlights at night in Greensburg

A wind farm does not grow wind like a farm that grows food! A wind farm is a place with wind turbines that use the wind to make electricity. During 2009 and 2010, Greensburg received 10 of these wind turbines to help the town become the "greenest" town in the USA.

Kansas is in the Midwest. That's in the middle of the United States. It is a very good place for a wind farm because the ground is flat. There are very few mountains and hills. And there is a lot of wind. Sometimes it is so windy that there are tornadoes like the one that destroyed Greensburg! The wind turbines on the wind farms in Greensburg make enough energy for 4,000 homes. That shows that being "green" can help make energy and save money.

EVALUATE
What are some other ways that the energy from wind could possibly be used in Kansas?

Wind turbines use the wind to make electricity.

Back in 2009, Greensburg had a competition for the best eco-home. The houses needed to be as cheap to build as possible and "green." Meadowlark House won the competition. The windows are low down on the southern side of the house. In the winter, the sunlight keeps the house warm. In the summer, the sun is higher in the sky. This means that not so much light can come in through the windows, so the house stays cool.

Meadowlark houses are made with large pieces of wood. The pieces are put together like the parts of a block game, so a house can be built quickly and cheaply. Many tourists who visit Greensburg now stay in these eco-homes. This way, visitors can understand what it is like to live in ecological homes like Meadowlark.

Meadowlark House

Every year the architecture students from Studio 804 at the University of Kansas build a building. After the 2007 tornado, the students and their teacher decided to build an ecological building in Greensburg.

In January 2008, the students began to make seven parts or modules of their building at the university in Lawrence, Kansas. Modules are built cheaply and quickly like cars in a factory. It's easy to move them, and it's easy to add new modules when you want to make a building bigger.

In May, the students moved the modules to Greensburg. The building was opened on May 4, 2008, exactly one year after the tornado hit the town.

Video Quest

Studio 804

Watch this video about the students of Studio 804. Why did they use modules for their building?

CHAPTER 4

An Exciting Place to Live

MANY PEOPLE HAVE HELPED MAKE GREENSBURG A BETTER PLACE TO LIVE.

In 2009, the actor Leonardo DiCaprio made a television program about Greensburg. The program tells the story of the most important things that happened to Greensburg before and after the tornado: what the town looked like before the tornado; the night that the tornado hit the town on May 4, 2007; the decision of the town to rebuild a "green" town; the ways that Greensburg changed after the tornado; and the people who helped it change.

Daniel Wallach and Catherine Hart are a husband and wife who have helped to make important changes in Greensburg, which is not far from where they live.

16

After the tornado hit in 2007, they wanted to help the town. Daniel and Catherine were the first members of GreensburgGreen, the group of people who first talked about making Greensburg "green." Daniel and Catherine said that it was important to remember that in the 19th century, people in Greensburg built windmills for energy, used water from rain, and built their houses to receive sunlight and stay warm in the winter. Being "green" is not new, it's a very old idea!

Daniel and Catherine helped Greensburg to begin building "eco-homes" where tourists can stay and learn about ecological living. Tourists make jobs because they spend money in the places they visit. They need places to stay and places to eat. In the past, many young people left Greensburg because there were no jobs in their town. But today, thanks to "green" tourism, there are more jobs, and more young people have decided to stay. Many of these young people want to try new ways of living, especially "green" ways of saving energy and money. Today Greensburg is one of the ten favorite small towns to visit in the United States. Visitors from all over the world come to visit and learn in this "green" town.

Daniel Wallach

In the fall of 2007 some teenage students from Greensburg decided to start a Green **Club**. They wanted to learn about how to be "green" and help their town to be ecological. Students in the Green Club told people in the town about the problems of using plastic bags; they asked them to recycle paper bags; and they sold ecological lights to help save energy.

Dustin Sypher is an artist who became a **blacksmith**. In the past, there were many blacksmiths everywhere, but today there are not very many. Dustin helped the Green Club make a bench[7] for their town from trees that were destroyed in the tornado and from old pieces of metal. Dustin and the Green Club showed that people can use things from the past to build a beautiful future.

Other people from Greensburg have helped make it a "greener" place.

[7]**bench:** a long seat for two or more people, usually made of wood or metal

In 2009, some people made a garden for the whole town. Anyone who wants to grow food can use the garden. It's also a great way for people to see their friends and to meet new people.

The Big **Well** was the most famous place in Greensburg. Since 1888 it has given water to the people of the town. But in 2007 the tornado covered the Big Well with rubble. The people of Greensburg rebuilt it, and in 2012 the Big Well opened again to visitors.

And finally, there's Ron Shank. Ron has sold cars in Greensburg for many years, but now he sells electric cars! He also rides a tricycle[8] to work!

[8] **tricycle:** a bicycle with three wheels, usually ridden by children

Video Quest

Insulation

Watch this video about one idea for controlling the temperature in a green building. What did the students use for **insulation**? Why?

CHAPTER 5

What Do You Think?

GREENSBURG HAS TAUGHT THE WORLD A LESSON ABOUT BEING "GREEN." WHAT DO YOU THINK ABOUT THE WAY PEOPLE IN GREENSBURG CHANGED THE TOWN?

The tornado made a lot of trouble for the people living in Greensburg. But what happened after that was an important lesson for the whole world. Greensburg tried something new: building a "green" town. The town made laws to make the environment safe.

Today, many tourists go to Greensburg to learn about ecological living. These visitors spend money in the town and help Greensburg to grow.

Cities like Paris, France can learn a lot from Greensburg.

Many of these tourists want to know more about the changes that happened in Greensburg. In this way, people from other parts of the world can learn to make their own lives better. They can learn to help the environment, too.

The tornado that destroyed Greensburg was terrible, but something good came from it. Think of something bad that happened to you in the past. What is something good that came from it later? What good might come from it in the future?

After You Read

True or False

Read the sentences and choose Ⓐ (True) or Ⓑ (False). If the book does not tell you, choose Ⓒ (Doesn't say).

1 It was a month before the people of Greensburg could return to their town after the tornado.
- Ⓐ True
- Ⓑ False
- Ⓒ Doesn't say

2 Everyone in Greensburg wanted to have a "green" town after the tornado.
- Ⓐ True
- Ⓑ False
- Ⓒ Doesn't say

3 Greensburg was the first city in the United States to use "green" streetlights in 2009.
- Ⓐ True
- Ⓑ False
- Ⓒ Doesn't say

4 Greensburg has 25 wind turbines.
- Ⓐ True
- Ⓑ False
- Ⓒ Doesn't say

5 Greensburg was the third "Eco-Town" to be built in the world.
- Ⓐ True
- Ⓑ False
- Ⓒ Doesn't say

6 The class of students that built a "green" building in Greensburg is called Studio 804.
- Ⓐ True
- Ⓒ False
- Ⓒ Doesn't say

7 There are five laws about building "green" in Greensburg.
- Ⓐ True
- Ⓑ False
- Ⓒ Doesn't say

8 Dan Rockhill is the teacher of the students of architecture at the University of Kansas.
- Ⓐ True
- Ⓑ False
- Ⓒ Doesn't say

Complete the Text

Use the words in the box to complete the sentences.

| Big Well | eco-home | wind farm |
| blacksmiths | streetlights | |

1 This can make enough energy for 4,000 homes: _____

2 Today there are not many of these people who use metal to make things: _____

3 A place to live for some of the people of Greensburg and tourists: _____

4 This was built in 1888: _____

5 These are what now save a lot of energy at night in Greensburg: _____

ANALYZE
Imagine that you are going to go to Greensburg to live for a week to study how the town has become "green." What would you like to study there? Why?

Answer Key

Words to Know, page 4
① Wind turbines ② tornado ③ eco-home ④ destroy

Words to Know, page 5
① environment ② Recycling ③ Insulation ④ energy
⑤ "Green" ⑥ ecological

Predict, page 5
Answers will vary.

Video Quest, page 9
The tornado was 2.7 kilometers wide. Its winds blew at 330 kilometers per hour.

Apply, page 11 *Answers will vary.*

Evaluate, page 13 *Answers will vary.*

Video Quest, page 15
Modules are built somewhere else and put together at the location to make a building.

Video Quest, page 19
Suggested Answer: The students used wet newspaper to fill the spaces in the walls. The building will use less energy.

True or False, page 22
① B ② B ③ A ④ B ⑤ C ⑥ A ⑦ C ⑧ A

Complete the Text, page 23
① wind farm ② blacksmiths ③ eco-home ④ Big Well
⑤ streetlights

Analyze, page 23 *Answers will vary.*

24